RECIPE SOUP MIX

RECIPE SECRETS®

PUBLICATIONS INTERNATIONAL, LTD.

This edition published by Publications International, Ltd., 7373 N. Cicero Ave., Lincolnwood, IL 60646.

Project Director: Anna Marie Cesario, Manager-Consumer Services
Project Coordinators: Julie Nolan, Home Economist
Mindy Sweetwood, Home Economist

Recipe Development: The Lipton Kitchens
Test Kitchen Assistant: Yolanda Bernal-Bernal
Project Administrator: Michelle Febres

Photography: Sacco Productions Limited, Chicago

Pictured on the front cover: Three Bean Salsa (*page 26*).

Pictured on the back cover (*from top to bottom*): Mediterranean Feta Dip (*page 8*), Polenta Triangles (*page 10*), Oven-Roasted Vegetables (*page 22*) and Golden Glazed Flank Steak (*page 38*).

ISBN: 0-7853-1119-X

Manufactured in U.S.A.

8 7 6 5 4 3 2 1

The **Lipton** Kitchens
™ Taste Tested Recipes

RECIPE SECRETS®

Anytime Appetizers

Can't Get Enough Chicken Wings

12 chicken wings (about 2 pounds)
½ cup butter or margarine, melted
1 envelope Lipton Recipe Secrets Savory Herb with Garlic Soup Mix
1 teaspoon cayenne pepper sauce* (optional)

Cut tips off chicken wings (save tips for soup). Cut chicken wings in half at joint. Deep fry, bake or broil until golden brown and crunchy.

In medium bowl, blend butter, savory herb with garlic soup mix and cayenne pepper sauce. Add hot cooked chicken wings; toss until coated. Serve, if desired, over greens with cut-up celery.   Makes 24 appetizers

*Use more or less according to taste desired.

Entertaining Suggestions: Serve with Mini Mexican Meatballs (page 13) and Roasted Red Pepper Dip (page 20).

Mediterranean Feta Dip

1 envelope Lipton Recipe Secrets Vegetable Soup Mix
1 container (16 ounces) sour cream
4 ounces feta or blue cheese, crumbled
½ cup seeded diced cucumber
2 tablespoons chopped red onion
½ teaspoon dried oregano leaves, crushed (optional)

In medium bowl, thoroughly blend all ingredients; cover and chill.

Makes about 2½ cups dip

Dipper Suggestions: Serve with assorted fresh vegetables, pita bread triangles and pitted ripe olives.

Buffalo Wings

24 chicken wings (about 4 pounds)
1 envelope Lipton Recipe Secrets Golden Onion or Onion Soup Mix
½ cup butter or margarine, melted
2 tablespoons white vinegar
2 tablespoons water
2 cloves garlic
1½ to 2 teaspoons ground red pepper
1 teaspoon ground cumin (optional)

Cut tips off chicken wings (save tips for a soup). Cut chicken wings in half at joint.

In food processor or blender, process golden onion soup mix, butter, vinegar, water, garlic, pepper and cumin until blended; set aside.

Broil chicken 12 minutes or until brown, turning after 6 minutes. Brush with ½ of the soup mixture, then broil 2 minutes or until crisp. Turn, then brush with remaining soup mixture and broil an additional minute.

Makes 48 appetizers

Entertaining Suggestions: Serve with Wish-Bone Chunky Blue Cheese Dressing and celery sticks, Caponata Spread (page 14) and Zesty Bruschetta (page 14).

Spinach Rice Balls

1½ cups cooked rice
 1 package (10 ounces) frozen chopped spinach, cooked and well drained
 ½ cup shredded mozzarella cheese (about 1½ ounces)
 ⅓ cup plain dry bread crumbs
 2 eggs, slightly beaten
 ¼ cup grated Parmesan cheese
 ¼ cup milk
 1 teaspoon Dijon-style, country Dijon-style or brown prepared mustard
 1 envelope Lipton Recipe Secrets Golden Onion Soup Mix

Preheat oven to 375°F.

In medium bowl, combine all ingredients; shape into 1-inch balls. On well-greased baking sheet, arrange rice balls and bake 20 minutes or until golden. Serve warm and, if desired, with assorted mustards.

Makes about 2 dozen rice balls

Entertaining Suggestions: Serve with Golden Chicken Nuggets (page 16), Mini Mexican Meatballs (page 13) and Easy Italian Turnovers (recipe below) for an international appetizer buffet.

Easy Italian Turnovers

 1 envelope Lipton Recipe Secrets Italian Herb with Tomato Soup Mix
 1 pound ground beef
 ¾ cup chopped onion
 ½ cup water
 ½ cup fresh bread crumbs
 2 tablespoons grated Parmesan cheese
 1 package (15 ounces) refrigerated pie crust for 2 crusts (9 inches *each*)

Preheat oven to 350°F.

In medium bowl, combine all ingredients except pie crust; set aside.

Open pie crusts; cut each into quarters to make 8 triangles. Place ¼ cup beef mixture on bottom half of each triangle. Fold over top half and seal edges using fork. Arrange on baking sheet and bake 25 minutes or until pastry is golden brown.

Makes 8 turnovers

♦ Also terrific with Lipton Recipe Secrets Savory Herb with Garlic or Onion-Mushroom Soup Mix.

Menu Suggestion: Serve with your favorite Lipton Soup and steamed fresh vegetables.

Polenta Triangles

  3 cups cold water
  1 cup yellow cornmeal
  1 envelope Lipton Recipe Secrets Golden Onion or Onion Soup Mix
  1 can (4 ounces) mild chopped green chilies, drained
  ½ cup thawed frozen *or* drained canned whole kernel corn
  ⅓ cup finely chopped roasted red peppers
  ½ cup shredded sharp Cheddar cheese (about 2 ounces)

In 3-quart saucepan, bring water to a boil over high heat. With wire whisk, stir in cornmeal, then golden onion soup mix. Reduce heat to low and simmer uncovered, stirring constantly, 25 minutes or until thickened. Stir in chilies, corn and roasted red peppers. Spread into lightly greased 9-inch square baking pan; sprinkle with cheese. Let stand 20 minutes or until firm; cut into triangles. Serve at room temperature or heat in oven at 350°F for 5 minutes or until warm.   Makes about 24 triangles

Menu Suggestion: Serve as an hors d'oeuvre or first course.

Taco Dip

  1 envelope Lipton Recipe Secrets Onion Soup Mix
  1 container (16 ounces) sour cream
  1 package (8 ounces) cream cheese, softened
  ¼ pound ground beef, cooked, drained and crumbled
  ¾ cup shredded Monterey Jack or Cheddar cheese (about 3 ounces), divided
     Shredded lettuce
     Chopped tomato
     Tortilla chips

Preheat oven to 350°F.

In shallow 1-quart casserole, combine onion soup mix, sour cream, cream cheese, ground beef and ½ cup shredded Monterey Jack cheese. Sprinkle remaining ¼ cup cheese over top. Bake 30 minutes or until heated through. Top with lettuce and tomato and serve with tortilla chips.

                    Makes about 3½ cups dip

♦ Also terrific with Lipton Recipe Secrets Onion-Mushroom or Italian Herb with Tomato Soup Mix.

Entertaining Suggestions: Serve with Zesty Bruschetta (page 14) and Party Peanut Crisp (page 21).

Top to bottom: Mediterranean Feta Dip (page 8), Polenta Triangles

Onion-Potato Pancakes

1 pound all-purpose potatoes, peeled
2 large eggs, beaten
1 envelope Lipton Recipe Secrets Onion or Savory Herb with
    Garlic Soup Mix
2 tablespoons olive or vegetable oil, divided

In food processor with grating attachment or with hand grater, coarsely grate potatoes; drain on several layers of paper towels until almost dry. In medium bowl, combine potatoes, eggs and onion soup mix.

In 12-inch nonstick skillet, heat 1 tablespoon oil over medium-high heat and drop ½ of the potato mixture by rounded tablespoons into skillet. Cook 1 minute on each side or until golden brown, pressing down lightly with spatula when turning; drain on paper towels. Repeat with remaining 1 tablespoon oil and remaining potato mixture.

Makes about 24 potato pancakes

Variation: Stir in 1 can (4 ounces) chopped green chilies, drained, *or* 1 can (7 ounces) corn, drained, with potatoes.

Serving Suggestion: Serve with applesauce and sour cream or plain yogurt.

Warm Broccoli 'n Cheddar Dip

1 envelope Lipton Recipe Secrets Vegetable Soup Mix
1 container (16 ounces) sour cream
1 package (10 ounces) frozen chopped broccoli or spinach, thawed and
    squeezed dry
1 cup shredded Cheddar cheese (about 4 ounces), divided

Preheat oven to 350°F.

In 1-quart casserole, combine vegetable soup mix, sour cream, broccoli and ¾ cup cheese. Top with remaining ¼ cup cheese. Bake 30 minutes or until heated through.

Makes about 3 cups dip

Dipper Suggestions: Serve with fresh vegetables, bread sticks or crackers.

Mini Mexican Meatballs

1 envelope Lipton Recipe Secrets Onion or Beefy Onion Soup Mix
1½ pounds ground beef
1 egg
1 tablespoon cornmeal (optional)
1 can (4 ounces) chopped green chilies, undrained, divided
1 can (14½ ounces) whole peeled tomatoes, undrained and chopped
1 teaspoon ground cumin (optional)

In medium bowl, combine onion soup mix, ground beef, egg, cornmeal and 1 tablespoon chilies; shape into 1-inch meatballs. In 12-inch skillet, brown meatballs over medium-high heat; drain. Add tomatoes, remaining chilies and cumin. Bring to a boil over high heat; cook 1 minute. Reduce heat to low and simmer covered 8 minutes or until meatballs are done. Serve, if desired, with tortilla chips.   Makes about 4 dozen meatballs

Entertaining Suggestions: Serve with Golden Chicken Nuggets (page 16) and White Pizza Dip (page 18).

The Famous Lipton California Dip

1 envelope Lipton Recipe Secrets Onion Soup Mix
1 container (16 ounces) sour cream

In small bowl, blend onion soup mix with sour cream; cover and chill.
Makes about 2 cups dip

Note: For creamier dip, add more sour cream.

Variations:
SENSATIONAL SPINACH DIP: Add 1 package (10 ounces) frozen chopped spinach, thawed and squeezed dry.

CALIFORNIA SEAFOOD DIP: Add 1 cup finely chopped cooked clams, crabmeat or shrimp, ¼ cup chili sauce and 1 tablespoon horseradish.

CALIFORNIA BACON DIP: Add ⅓ cup crumbled cooked bacon or bacon bits.

CALIFORNIA BLUE CHEESE DIP: Add ¼ pound crumbled blue cheese and ¼ cup finely chopped walnuts.

Dipper Suggestions: Serve with assorted cut-up fresh vegetables, crackers, bread sticks or toasted pita bread wedges.

Zesty Bruschetta

**1 envelope Lipton Recipe Secrets Savory Herb with Garlic or Italian Herb
   with Tomato Soup Mix**
3 tablespoons olive or vegetable oil
1 loaf French or Italian bread (about 18 inches long), halved lengthwise
2 tablespoons shredded or grated Parmesan cheese

Preheat oven to 350°F.

Blend savory herb with garlic soup mix and oil. Brush onto bread, then
sprinkle with cheese. Bake 15 minutes. Slice, then serve.

Makes 1 loaf, about 18 pieces

Entertaining Suggestions: Serve with Onion-Potato Pancakes (page 12)
and Warm Broccoli 'n Cheddar Dip (page 12).

Caponata Spread

1½ tablespoons olive or vegetable oil
1 medium eggplant, diced (about 4 cups)
1 medium onion, chopped
1½ cups water, divided
1 envelope Lipton Recipe Secrets Savory Herb with Garlic Soup Mix
2 tablespoons chopped fresh parsley (optional)
Salt and pepper to taste
Pita chips or thinly sliced Italian or French bread

In 10-inch nonstick skillet, heat oil over medium heat and cook eggplant
with onion 3 minutes. Add ½ cup water. Reduce heat to low and simmer
covered 3 minutes. Stir in savory herb with garlic soup mix blended with
remaining 1 cup water. Bring to a boil over high heat. Reduce heat to low
and simmer uncovered, stirring occasionally, 20 minutes. Stir in parsley, salt
and pepper. Serve with pita chips.   Makes about 4 cups spread

♦ Also terrific with Lipton Recipe Secrets Italian Herb with Tomato or
   Onion-Mushroom Soup Mix.

Entertaining Suggestions: Serve with Easy Italian Turnovers (page 9) and
Party Peanut Crisp (page 21).

*Left to right: Zesty Bruschetta,
Caponata Spread*

Golden Chicken Nuggets

1 envelope Lipton Recipe Secrets Onion-Mushroom Soup Mix
¾ cup plain dry bread crumbs
1½ pounds boneless skinless chicken breasts, cut into 1-inch pieces
3 tablespoons butter or margarine, melted

Preheat oven to 400°F.

Combine onion-mushroom soup mix with bread crumbs. Dip chicken in bread crumb mixture, coating well. In lightly greased 13×9-inch baking or roasting pan, arrange chicken in single layer. Drizzle with butter. Bake 10 minutes or until chicken is done, turning once.

Makes about 2 dozen nuggets

Note: Recipe can be doubled.

♦ Also terrific with Lipton Recipe Secrets Onion, Golden Onion or Savory Herb with Garlic Soup Mix.

Variation:
CAJUN-STYLE CHICKEN NUGGETS: Add 1½ teaspoons chili powder, 1 teaspoon ground cumin and ¼ teaspoon red pepper to bread crumb mixture.

Menu Suggestion: Serve with a mixed green salad and French fries.

Lipton Recipe Secrets Dip Recipes

1 envelope Lipton Recipe Secrets Beefy Onion, Golden Onion, Onion, Onion-Mushroom, Vegetable, Savory Herb with Garlic, Italian Herb with Tomato or Golden Herb with Lemon Soup Mix
1 container (16 ounces) sour cream

In small bowl, blend soup mix with sour cream. Cover and chill.

Makes about 2 cups dip

Note: For creamier dip, add more sour cream.

Serving Suggestions: For a terrific taste, stir in crumbled cooked bacon or bacon bits, shredded carrots or chopped radishes. Serve with potato chips, crackers or assorted fresh vegetables, such as celery or carrot sticks, green bell pepper strips or cherry tomatoes.

Baked Vegetable & Seafood Won Tons

     1 envelope Lipton Recipe Secrets Vegetable Soup Mix
     1 container (15 ounces) ricotta cheese
    ½ pound imitation crabmeat, chopped *or* 1½ cups chopped cooked shrimp
    ¼ teaspoon garlic powder
    ⅛ teaspoon ground black pepper
    40 refrigerated or thawed frozen won ton wrappers
       Water
     1 tablespoon olive or vegetable oil

Preheat oven to 350°F.

In medium bowl, combine vegetable soup mix, cheese, crabmeat, garlic powder and pepper. Place 1 tablespoon ricotta mixture on center of each won ton. Brush edges with water; fold each corner into center and press to seal. Arrange seam-side-down on lightly greased baking sheet; brush won tons with oil. Bake 25 minutes or until crisp and golden brown, turning once.

Makes 40 won tons

Note: Cover unbaked won tons with a damp cloth until ready to bake; brush with oil.

Entertaining Suggestions: Serve with Polenta Triangles (page 10) and Caponata Spread (page 14).

Extra Special Spinach Dip

     1 envelope Lipton Recipe Secrets Vegetable Soup Mix
     1 container (16 ounces) sour cream
    ½ cup mayonnaise
    ½ teaspoon lemon juice
     1 package (10 ounces) frozen chopped spinach, thawed and squeezed dry
     1 can (8 ounces) water chestnuts, drained and chopped

In medium bowl, blend vegetable soup mix, sour cream, mayonnaise and lemon juice. Stir in spinach and water chestnuts; chill.

Makes about 3 cups dip

Variations: Stir in 2 tablespoons chopped green onions, radishes or crumbled blue cheese; or omit water chestnuts and add 1 cup chopped apple.

White Pizza Dip

1 envelope Lipton Recipe Secrets Savory Herb with Garlic Soup Mix
1 container (8 ounces) sour cream
1 cup (8 ounces) ricotta cheese
1 cup shredded mozzarella cheese (about 3 ounces), divided
1 jar (4½ ounces) sliced mushrooms, drained (optional)
¼ cup (1 ounce) chopped pepperoni (optional)
1 loaf Italian bread, sliced and toasted

Preheat oven to 350°F.

In shallow 1-quart casserole, combine savory herb with garlic soup mix, sour cream, ricotta cheese, ¾ cup shredded mozzarella, mushrooms and pepperoni. Sprinkle with remaining ¼ cup cheese. Bake 30 minutes or until heated through. Serve with bread.   Makes about 2 cups dip

Variation:
TRADITIONAL-STYLE PIZZA DIP: Use 1 envelope Lipton Recipe Secrets Italian Herb with Tomato Soup Mix.

> **Entertaining Suggestions:** Serve with Golden Chicken Nuggets (page 16) and Onion-Potato Pancakes (page 12).

Snappy Party Snacks

8 cups oven-toasted rice, corn and/or wheat cereal
1 cup unsalted dry roasted mixed nuts
1 envelope Lipton Recipe Secrets Onion or Savory Herb with Garlic Soup Mix
½ cup butter or margarine, melted

Preheat oven to 300°F.

In large bowl, combine cereal, nuts and onion soup mix. Add butter and toss thoroughly. Turn onto baking sheet and bake 10 minutes.
                    Makes about 9 cups party snacks

Variation: For extra fun party snacks, after baking add any combination of the following to equal 2 cups: bite-size chewy real fruit snacks, semi-sweet chocolate chips, raisins, shredded coconut, small pretzels and mini-marshmallows.

> **Menu Suggestion:** Serve with Fresco Marinated Chicken (page 64) and cole slaw or potato salad.

White Pizza Dip

Roasted Red Pepper Dip

    1 envelope Lipton Recipe Secrets Onion Soup Mix
    1 package (8 ounces) cream cheese, softened
    1 jar (7 ounces) roasted red peppers packed in oil, undrained
    ½ teaspoon dried basil leaves, crushed (optional)
    ¼ teaspoon dried oregano leaves, crushed (optional)

In food processor or blender, combine all ingredients until smooth. Cover and chill at least 2 hours.   Makes about 2 cups dip

♦ Also terrific with Lipton Recipe Secrets Onion-Mushroom or Savory Herb with Garlic Soup Mix.

Dipper Suggestions: Use mozzarella sticks, bread sticks, sliced pepperoni, cooked tortellini, pitted ripe olives or cherry tomatoes.

Four Cheese Spread

    1 package (8 ounces) cream cheese, softened
    1 cup shredded Swiss cheese (about 4 ounces)
    1 cup shredded Fontina or Monterey Jack cheese (about 3 ounces)
    ½ cup sour cream
    ¼ cup grated Parmesan cheese
    ¼ cup finely chopped fresh basil leaves *or* 1½ teaspoons dried basil leaves, crushed
    1 tablespoon finely chopped parsley
    1 tablespoon lemon juice
    1 envelope Lipton Recipe Secrets Vegetable Soup Mix

Line 4-cup mold or bowl with waxed paper or dampened cheese cloth; set aside.

With food processor or electric mixer, combine all ingredients until smooth. Pack into prepared mold; cover and chill. To serve, unmold onto serving platter and remove waxed paper. Garnish, if desired, with additional chopped parsley and basil.   Makes about 3½ cups spread

Serving Suggestions: Serve with assorted crackers, bagel chips or cucumber slices.

Party Peanut Crisp

1 envelope Lipton Recipe Secrets Onion Soup Mix
¾ cup all-purpose flour
¾ cup butter or margarine, softened
½ cup firmly packed brown sugar
1 egg
1 teaspoon ground cumin (optional)
1 cup spoon-size shredded wheat cereal
1 cup natural whole almonds
1 cup unsalted peanuts

Preheat oven to 350°F.

Line jelly-roll pan with aluminum foil; spray with no stick cooking spray and set aside. In large bowl with electric mixer, combine onion soup mix, flour, butter, brown sugar, egg and cumin until well blended. Stir in remaining ingredients; spread into prepared pan. Bake 25 minutes or until golden brown. Cool completely on wire rack. To serve, break into pieces. Store in airtight container up to 2 weeks.

Makes 1½ pounds (40 pieces) peanut crisp

Entertaining Suggestions: Serve as an appetizer with Mediterranean Feta Dip (page 8) and Polenta Triangles (page 10).

♦ Vegetable Crudités ♦

Offer fresh vegetables in a basket or clean clay flower pot lined with the outer leaves of fresh lettuce or cabbage. To hold a dip, carefully hollow out a cabbage head or a large bell pepper. The dip and cut vegetables may be prepared a day ahead and stored, tightly wrapped, in the refrigerator.

Savory Side Dishes

Oven-Roasted Vegetables

  1 envelope Lipton Recipe Secrets Savory Herb with Garlic Soup Mix
1½ pounds assorted fresh vegetables*
  2 tablespoons olive or vegetable oil**

Preheat oven to 450°F.

In large plastic bag or bowl, add all ingredients. Close bag and shake, or toss in bowl, until vegetables are evenly coated. Empty vegetables into 13×9-inch baking or roasting pan; discard bag. Bake, stirring once, 20 minutes or until vegetables are tender.   Makes 4 (½-cup) servings

*Use any combination of the following, sliced: zucchini, yellow squash, red or green bell peppers, carrots, celery and mushrooms.

**Substitution: Spray pan lightly with no stick cooking spray and replace oil with 2 tablespoons water.

♦ Also terrific with Lipton Recipe Secrets Golden Herb with Lemon, Italian Herb with Tomato, Onion or Golden Onion Soup Mix.

Menu Suggestion: Serve with roasted chicken and a tossed green salad.

Oven-Roasted Vegetables

Broccoli Casserole with Crumb Topping

2 slices day-old white bread, coarsely crumbled (about 1¼ cups)
½ cup shredded mozzarella cheese (about 1½ ounces)
2 tablespoons chopped fresh parsley (optional)
2 tablespoons olive or vegetable oil, divided
1 small clove garlic, finely chopped
6 cups broccoli flowerets and/or cauliflowerets
1 envelope Lipton Recipe Secrets Onion Soup Mix
1 cup water
1 large tomato, diced

In small bowl, combine bread crumbs, cheese, parsley, 1 tablespoon oil and garlic; set aside.

In 12-inch skillet, heat remaining 1 tablespoon oil over medium heat and cook broccoli, stirring frequently, 2 minutes. Stir in onion soup mix blended with water. Bring to a boil over high heat. Reduce heat to low and simmer uncovered, stirring occasionally, 8 minutes or until broccoli is almost tender. Add tomato; simmer an additional 2 minutes. Spoon vegetable mixture into 2-quart broilerproof baking dish; top with bread crumb mixture. Broil 1½ minutes or until crumbs are golden and cheese is melted.

Makes about 6 servings

Menu Suggestion: Serve with Chicken with Golden Caper Sauce (page 80) and fresh fruit.

◆ Shortcuts ◆

When a recipe calls for fresh herbs, you can usually substitute dried. For each tablespoon fresh, use 1 teaspoon dried.

Peel garlic cloves quickly and easily by placing on a cutting board and hitting firmly with the flat side of a large knife.

Grate soft cheese easily by first popping it in the freezer for 15 minutes.

◆

Savory Skillet Potatoes

1½ pounds all-purpose potatoes, diced
 1 large onion, thinly sliced
 1 envelope Lipton Recipe Secrets Savory Herb with Garlic Soup Mix
 2 tablespoons olive or vegetable oil

In large bowl, toss potatoes, onion and savory herb with garlic soup mix until potatoes are well coated.

In 12-inch nonstick skillet, heat oil over medium-high heat and cook potato mixture, covered, 5 minutes. Remove cover and cook, stirring frequently, an additional 10 minutes or until potatoes are tender.

Makes about 6 servings

♦ Also terrific with Lipton Recipe Secrets Onion or Italian Herb with Tomato Soup Mix.

Menu Suggestion: Serve with scrambled eggs and toast or English muffins.

Orzo Risotto

 1 tablespoon butter or margarine
 1 medium clove garlic, finely chopped
1½ cups uncooked orzo pasta
 1 envelope Lipton Recipe Secrets Onion or Onion-Mushroom Soup Mix
2¾ cups water
1½ cups milk
 ¼ cup frozen peas, thawed
 ¼ cup grated Parmesan cheese

In 3-quart heavy saucepan, melt butter over medium heat and cook garlic until almost golden. Add orzo and stir until coated with butter. Stir in onion soup mix blended with water. Bring to a boil over high heat. Reduce heat to low and simmer covered 8 minutes. Stir in milk and peas and simmer, stirring frequently, until heated through, about 1 minute. Stir in cheese. Serve immediately.

Makes about 4 cups

Menu Suggestion: Serve with broiled pork chops or chicken cutlets and melon wedges.

Lipton California Mashed Potatoes

    2 pounds all-purpose potatoes, peeled, if desired, and cut into chunks
      Water
    2 tablespoons chopped fresh parsley (optional)
    1 envelope Lipton Recipe Secrets Onion Soup Mix
    ¾ cup milk, heated to boiling
    ½ cup sour cream

In 3-quart saucepan, cover potatoes with water. Bring to a boil over high heat. Reduce heat to low and simmer 20 minutes or until potatoes are very tender; drain. Return potatoes to saucepan. Mash potatoes. Stir in parsley and onion soup mix blended with hot milk and sour cream.

                                          Makes about 8 servings

♦ Also terrific with Lipton Recipe Secrets Golden Onion, Golden Herb with Lemon or Savory Herb with Garlic Soup Mix.

Menu Suggestion: Serve with pork chops, beef or chicken and your favorite vegetable.

Three Bean Salsa

    1 envelope Lipton Recipe Secrets Savory Herb with Garlic Soup Mix
    ½ cup water
    1 large tomato, chopped
    1 cup drained canned cannellini or red kidney beans
    1 cup drained canned black or pinto beans
    1 cup drained canned chick-peas or garbanzo beans
    2 teaspoons white or white wine vinegar (optional)

In 12-inch skillet, blend savory herb with garlic soup mix with water. Bring to a boil over high heat; stir in tomato. Reduce heat to low and simmer 3 minutes. Stir in beans and simmer 3 minutes or until heated through. Stir in vinegar. Garnish, if desired, with chopped fresh parsley or cilantro.

                                          Makes about 4 cups bean salsa

Menu Suggestion: Serve as a side dish or topping with grilled poultry, beef, lamb or pork.

Three Bean Salsa

Layered Vegetable Bake

2 slices day-old white bread, crumbled
2 tablespoons chopped fresh parsley (optional)
2 tablespoons butter or margarine, melted
1 large all-purpose potato (about ½ pound), thinly sliced
1 large yellow or red bell pepper, sliced
1 envelope Lipton Recipe Secrets Savory Herb with Garlic or
   Golden Onion Soup Mix
1 large tomato, sliced

Preheat oven to 375°F.

Spray 1½-quart round casserole or baking dish with no stick cooking spray. In small bowl, combine bread crumbs, parsley and butter; set aside.

In prepared baking dish, arrange potato slices; top with yellow pepper. Sprinkle with savory herb with garlic soup mix. Arrange tomato slices over pepper, overlapping slightly. Sprinkle with bread crumb mixture. Cover with aluminum foil and bake 45 minutes. Remove foil and continue baking 15 minutes or until vegetables are tender.   Makes about 6 servings

Menu Suggestion: Serve with your favorite pork, beef or lamb roast and parslied rice.

Warm Potato Salad

2 tablespoons olive or vegetable oil
1 large red or green bell pepper, diced
1 medium onion, diced
2 pounds all-purpose potatoes, peeled, if desired, and cut into ½-inch pieces
1 envelope Lipton Recipe Secrets Savory Herb with Garlic Soup Mix
1 cup water
2 tablespoons red wine vinegar
1 teaspoon Dijon-style mustard

In 12-inch skillet, heat oil over medium heat and cook red pepper and onion, stirring frequently, 5 minutes. Add potatoes and savory herb with garlic soup mix blended with water. Bring to a boil over high heat. Reduce heat to low and simmer covered, stirring occasionally, 15 minutes or until potatoes are tender. Stir in vinegar and mustard. Serve warm.

Makes about 6 servings

Menu Suggestion: Serve with hamburgers, hot dogs or chicken and corn-on-the-cob.

Layered Vegetable Bake

Buffalo Potatoes

**1 envelope Lipton Recipe Secrets Savory Herb with Garlic or
  Onion Soup Mix**
⅓ cup butter or margarine, melted
2 to 4 tablespoons cayenne pepper sauce
**2 pounds baking potatoes, sliced lengthwise into wedges
  Wish-Bone Chunky Blue Cheese Dressing**

Preheat oven to 450°F.

In 13×9-inch baking or roasting pan, blend savory herb with garlic soup mix, butter and pepper sauce. Add potatoes and turn to coat. Bake, stirring occasionally, 45 minutes or until potatoes are crisp. Serve with dressing.

Makes about 4 servings

Entertaining Suggestions: Serve with Can't Get Enough Chicken Wings (page 6) and Party Peanut Crisp (page 21).

Onion-Roasted Potatoes

1 envelope Lipton Recipe Secrets Onion Soup Mix
2 pounds all-purpose potatoes, cut into large chunks
⅓ cup olive or vegetable oil

Preheat oven to 450°F.

In large plastic bag or bowl, add all ingredients. Close bag and shake, or toss in bowl, until potatoes are evenly coated. Empty potatoes into 13×9-inch baking or roasting pan; discard bag. Bake, stirring occasionally, 40 minutes or until potatoes are tender and golden brown. Garnish, if desired, with chopped fresh parsley.

Makes about 8 servings

♦ Also terrific with Lipton Recipe Secrets Onion-Mushroom, Savory Herb with Garlic or Italian Herb with Tomato Soup Mix.

Menu Suggestion: Serve with your favorite beef, pork or chicken recipe and steamed vegetables.

*Clockwise from top:
Onion-Roasted Potatoes,
Mashed Potatoes Florentine (page 32),
Buffalo Potatoes*

Mashed Potatoes Florentine

  2 **pounds all-purpose potatoes, peeled, if desired, and cut into chunks**
    Water
  7 **cups trimmed, washed and drained fresh spinach or kale leaves (about**
     ½ pound)*
  1 **envelope Lipton Recipe Secrets Savory Herb with Garlic Soup Mix**
  ½ **cup milk**
  ¼ **cup butter or margarine**

In 3-quart saucepan, cover potatoes with water. Bring to a boil over high heat. Reduce heat to low and simmer 20 minutes or until potatoes are very tender. Stir in spinach and cook an additional 2 minutes or until spinach is wilted; drain. Return potatoes and spinach to saucepan; mash potatoes with spinach.

Meanwhile, in small saucepan, heat savory herb with garlic soup mix, milk and butter over low heat, stirring occasionally, until butter is melted. Stir into potato mixture.   Makes about 8 servings

*Substitution: Use 1 package (10 ounces) frozen chopped spinach, thawed and drained.

♦ Also terrific with Lipton Recipe Secrets Golden Onion or Golden Herb with Lemon Soup Mix.

Menu Suggestion: Serve with Cornish hens, roasted chicken or steak.

Green Bean Tart

  1 **refrigerated pie crust or pastry for single-crust pie**
  1 **egg yolk (optional)**
  2 **tablespoons water (optional)**
  1 **envelope Lipton Recipe Secrets Vegetable Soup Mix**
  ¼ **cup milk**
  ¼ **cup grated Swiss or white Cheddar cheese (about 2 ounces)**
  1 **egg**
  8 **ounces fresh green beans, cooked and drained**

Preheat oven to 375°F. On lightly floured cookie sheet, unfold pie crust. Fold crust edges over 1 inch to form rim. Brush with egg yolk beaten with water. Bake 9 minutes; set aside. In medium bowl, blend vegetable soup mix, milk, cheese and 1 egg. Arrange green beans on prepared crust; evenly pour soup mixture over beans. Bake 15 minutes or until crust is golden and egg is set.
                    Makes 1 tart

Menu Suggestion: Serve as an hors d'oeuvre, first course or side dish.

Orzo Casserole

    2 tablespoons butter or margarine
    1 clove garlic, finely chopped
1½ cups uncooked orzo pasta
    1 envelope Lipton Recipe Secrets Onion or Onion-Mushroom Soup Mix
3¼ cups water
    6 ounces shiitake or white mushrooms, sliced
    ¼ cup chopped fresh parsley

In 3-quart heavy saucepan, melt butter over medium heat and cook garlic with orzo, stirring constantly, 2½ minutes or until golden. Stir in onion soup mix blended with water. Bring to a boil over high heat. Reduce heat to low and simmer covered 10 minutes. Add mushrooms; do not stir. Simmer covered 10 minutes. Stir in parsley. Turn into serving bowl. *Liquid will not be totally absorbed.* Let stand 10 minutes or until liquid is absorbed.

Makes about 10 (½-cup) servings

Variation:
SAVORY ORZO CASSEROLE: Increase water to 4 cups and use Lipton Recipe Secrets Savory Herb with Garlic Soup Mix.

Menu Suggestion: Serve with your favorite ham, pork, lamb or beef recipe.

Golden Herb Stuffing

    2 tablespoons butter or margarine
    1 medium carrot, diced
    1 rib celery, diced
    1 small onion, finely chopped
    1 envelope Lipton Recipe Secrets Savory Herb with Garlic or
        Golden Herb with Lemon Soup Mix
    2 cups fresh bread crumbs
    ¼ cup milk or water
    ½ cup chopped walnuts or pecans (optional)

In 10-inch skillet, melt butter over medium heat and cook carrot, celery and onion, stirring occasionally, 4 minutes.

In medium bowl, combine vegetables with remaining ingredients; toss well. Makes enough stuffing for 1 roasting chicken, 2 Cornish hens, 8 pork chops or 8 fish fillets. Or, turn into 1-quart baking dish and bake covered at 375°F for 25 minutes. Remove cover and bake an additional 5 minutes or until top is lightly browned.

Makes 4 (½-cup) servings

Menu Suggestion: Serve as above with whole berry cranberry sauce and baked apples.

Couscous with Vegetables in Savory Broth

    2 tablespoons butter or margarine
    1 large onion, sliced
½ **cup dry white wine or water**
    1 cup sliced carrots
    1 medium zucchini, sliced
    1 small red or green bell pepper, sliced
    1 envelope Lipton Recipe Secrets Savory Herb with Garlic Soup Mix
    2 cups water
1⅓ **cups (8 ounces) couscous, cooked***

In 12-inch skillet, melt butter over medium heat and cook onion, stirring occasionally, 5 minutes or until golden. Add wine and boil over high heat 1 minute. Stir in carrots, zucchini, red pepper and savory herb with garlic soup mix blended with water. Bring to a boil over high heat. Reduce heat to low and simmer uncovered, stirring occasionally, 15 minutes. To serve, spoon over hot couscous.

                  Makes about 5 side-dish or 2 main-dish servings

***Variation:** Use hot cooked penne or ziti pasta.

Menu Suggestion: Serve with a mixed green salad and sliced fresh fruit drizzled with honey for dessert.

Skillet Corn Sauté

    1 envelope Lipton Recipe Secrets Savory Herb with Garlic Soup Mix
¾ **cup water**
    4 cups frozen *or* drained canned whole kernel corn
    1 medium red or green bell pepper, diced
    1 green onion, thinly sliced (optional)

In 10-inch skillet, blend savory herb with garlic soup mix and water. Stir in corn and red pepper. Bring to a boil over high heat. Reduce heat to low and simmer covered 5 minutes, stirring once. Stir in green onion.

                  Makes about 8 servings

Menu Suggestion: Serve with roasted chicken and Onion-Roasted Potatoes (page 30).

Couscous with Vegetables in Savory Broth

Onion Risotto

2 tablespoons olive or vegetable oil
1 cup uncooked arborio, regular or converted rice
4 cups boiling water, divided
1 envelope Lipton Recipe Secrets Onion Soup Mix

In heavy-duty medium saucepan, heat oil over medium-high heat and cook rice, stirring constantly, 3 minutes. Slowly add 1 cup boiling water and onion soup mix, stirring constantly. Reduce heat to low and simmer, stirring frequently, until water is absorbed. Continue adding boiling water, 1 cup at a time, stirring frequently, until rice is slightly creamy and just tender.

Makes about 4 (1-cup) servings

Note: Arborio rice is found in specialty food stores. This high-starch, shorter, fatter grain rice is used in risotto for its creamy texture.

Variation: Add 1 cup thawed frozen peas, corn, sliced carrots or green beans with last cup of boiling water.

♦ Also terrific with Lipton Recipe Secrets Savory Herb with Garlic or Golden Onion Soup Mix.

Menu Suggestion: Serve with beef, lamb, veal or pork and a fresh fruit salad.

Diner Skillet Potatoes

1½ pounds all-purpose potatoes, peeled and diced
2 large red and/or green bell peppers, chopped
1 envelope Lipton Recipe Secrets Onion Soup Mix
2 tablespoons olive or vegetable oil

In large bowl, combine potatoes, peppers and onion soup mix until well coated.

In 12-inch nonstick skillet, heat oil over medium heat and cook potato mixture, covered, stirring occasionally, 10 minutes. Uncover and cook, stirring occasionally, an additional 10 minutes or until tender.

Makes about 6 servings

Menu Suggestion: Serve with Pork Chops Piquante (page 74), a lettuce wedge with your favorite Wish-Bone Dressing and a vegetable.

Braised Cabbage & Apples

    2 tablespoons butter or margarine
    1 large red cooking apple (such as Rome or Golden Delicious), diced
    1 medium onion, sliced
    1 medium head green or red cabbage, thinly sliced (about 13 cups)
    1 envelope Lipton Recipe Secrets Savory Herb with Garlic Soup Mix
    1 cup water
  ½ cup apple juice

In 12-inch skillet, melt butter over medium heat and cook apple and onion, stirring frequently, 5 minutes. Add cabbage, then savory herb with garlic soup mix blended with water and apple juice. Bring to a boil over high heat. Reduce heat to low and simmer covered 25 minutes or until cabbage is tender.
Makes about 8 servings

♦ Also terrific with Lipton Recipe Secrets Golden Onion or Golden Herb with Lemon Soup Mix.

Menu Suggestion: Serve with Country-Style Pot Roast (page 73) or pork chops.

Confetti Rice Pilaf

    1 tablespoon butter or margarine
    1 cup uncooked converted white rice
    1 cup fresh *or* drained canned sliced mushrooms
    2 medium carrots, diced (about ½ cup)
    1 envelope Lipton Recipe Secrets Savory Herb with Garlic Soup Mix
  2¼ cups water

In large skillet, melt butter over medium-high heat and cook rice until golden. Stir in mushrooms, carrots and savory herb with garlic soup mix blended with water. Bring to a boil over high heat. Reduce heat to low and simmer covered 20 minutes or until rice is tender.
Makes about 6 servings

♦ Also terrific with Lipton Recipe Secrets Golden Herb with Lemon, Golden Onion, Onion-Mushroom or Onion Soup Mix.

Menu Suggestion: Serve with stir-fried chicken or beef.

Oven Entrées

Golden Glazed Flank Steak

    1 envelope Lipton Recipe Secrets Onion or Onion-Mushroom Soup Mix
    1 jar (12 ounces) apricot or peach preserves
 ½ cup water
    1 flank steak (about 2 pounds), cut into thin strips
    2 medium green, red and/or yellow bell peppers, sliced
      Hot cooked rice

In small bowl, combine onion soup mix, preserves and water; set aside. On broiling pan, arrange steak and peppers; top with soup mixture. Broil, turning once, until steak is done. Serve over hot rice.

Makes about 8 servings

Menu Suggestion: Serve with Lipton Iced Tea and fresh fruit topped with shredded coconut for dessert.

Golden Glazed Flank Steak

Fillets Stuffed with Crabmeat

    1 envelope Lipton Recipe Secrets Savory Herb with Garlic Soup Mix
    ½ cup fresh bread crumbs
    1 package (6 ounces) frozen crabmeat, thawed and well drained
    ½ cup water
    2 teaspoons lemon juice
    4 fish fillets (about 1 pound)
    1 tablespoon butter or margarine, melted

Preheat oven to 350°F.

In medium bowl, combine savory herb with garlic soup mix, bread crumbs, crabmeat, water and lemon juice.

Top fillets evenly with crabmeat mixture; roll up and secure with wooden toothpicks. Place in lightly greased 2-quart oblong baking dish. Brush fish with butter and bake 25 minutes or until fish flakes. Remove toothpicks before serving.   **Makes 4 servings**

♦ Also terrific with Lipton Recipe Secrets Golden Herb with Lemon or Golden Onion Soup Mix.

Menu Suggestion: Serve with hot cooked white rice tossed with sliced almonds and orange wedges for dessert.

California Meat Loaf

    1 envelope Lipton Recipe Secrets Onion Soup Mix
    2 pounds ground beef
    1 container (8 ounces) sour cream
    1 bag (6 ounces) unsalted potato chips, crushed (about 3 cups)
    2 eggs

Preheat oven to 350°F.

In large bowl, combine all ingredients. In 13×9-inch baking or roasting pan, shape into loaf. Bake 1 hour or until done. Let stand 10 minutes before serving.   **Makes about 8 servings**

♦ Also terrific with Lipton Recipe Secrets Italian Herb with Tomato, Onion-Mushroom or Beefy Onion Soup Mix.

Menu Suggestion: Serve with cooked carrots and mashed potatoes.

Hearty Beef Short Ribs

1 tablespoon olive or vegetable oil
4 pounds beef chuck short ribs, cut into 2-inch pieces
2 cups diced fennel or celery
3 medium carrots, diced (about 1 cup)
1 tablespoon finely chopped garlic
1 can (28 ounces) whole peeled tomatoes, undrained and chopped
1 envelope Lipton Recipe Secrets Onion or Beefy Onion Soup Mix
1 cup water
Parmesan Polenta, optional (recipe follows)

Preheat oven to 350°F.

In 6-quart Dutch oven or heavy-duty saucepan, heat oil over medium-high heat and brown short ribs in two batches. Remove and keep warm; reserve 1 tablespoon drippings. To reserved drippings, add fennel, carrots and garlic and cook over medium heat, stirring frequently, 2 minutes. Stir in tomatoes and onion soup mix blended with water. Return short ribs to Dutch oven; bring to a boil over high heat. Cover with ovenproof lid or aluminum foil, or turn into baking pan and bake covered 2 hours or until ribs are tender. Skim fat, if necessary. Serve with Parmesan Polenta.   Makes about 8 servings

PARMESAN POLENTA: In 5-quart saucepot, bring 6½ cups water and 1 teaspoon salt to a boil over high heat. Reduce heat to medium and with wire whisk, gradually stir in 1½ cups cornmeal. Reduce heat to low and simmer, stirring frequently, until mixture is very thick, about 15 minutes. Stir in ¾ cup grated Parmesan cheese. Makes about 4 cups.

Menu Suggestion: Serve with Lipton Iced Tea and your favorite ice cream for dessert.

Savory Chicken & Biscuits

2 tablespoons olive or vegetable oil
1 pound boneless skinless chicken breasts, cut into 1-inch pieces (about 2 cups)
1 medium onion, chopped
1 cup thinly sliced carrots
1 cup thinly sliced celery
1 envelope Lipton Recipe Secrets Savory Herb with Garlic Soup Mix
1 cup milk
1 package (10 ounces) refrigerated flaky buttermilk biscuits

Preheat oven to 400°F.

In 12-inch skillet, heat oil over medium-high heat and cook chicken, stirring occasionally, 5 minutes or until almost done. Stir in onion, carrots and celery; cook, stirring occasionally, 3 minutes. Stir in savory herb with garlic soup mix blended with milk. Bring to the boiling point over medium-high heat, stirring occasionally; cook 1 minute. Turn into lightly greased 2-quart casserole; arrange biscuits on top of chicken mixture with edges touching. Bake 10 minutes or until biscuits are golden brown.

Makes about 4 servings

◆ Also terrific with Lipton Recipe Secrets Golden Onion or Golden Herb with Lemon Soup Mix.

Menu Suggestion: Serve with a mixed green salad and Lipton Iced Tea.

◆ Plan-Ahead Tip ◆

Cook up a storm on weekends for "thaw and heat" weekday dinners. Freeze soups, stocks, meat loaf and baked goods. Simply defrost and heat for a speedy supper.

◆

Savory Chicken & Biscuits

Golden Glazed Chicken Breasts

  1 envelope Lipton Recipe Secrets Onion Soup Mix
  ⅔ cup apricot or peach preserves *or* ⅔ cup peach-apricot sauce
  ½ cup water
  1 pound boneless skinless chicken breast halves
  2 large red or green bell peppers, sliced
    Hot cooked rice

In small bowl, thoroughly combine onion soup mix, preserves and water; set aside.

In aluminum foil-lined broiler pan, arrange chicken breasts and peppers; top with soup mixture. Broil 10 minutes or until chicken is done, turning once. Serve over hot rice. **Makes about 4 servings**

♦ Also terrific with Lipton Recipe Secrets Golden Onion or Savory Herb with Garlic Soup Mix.

Menu Suggestion: Serve with a tomato and onion salad.

Citrus Shrimp Kabobs

  1 envelope Lipton Recipe Secrets Savory Herb with Garlic Soup Mix
  ¼ cup lemon or lime juice
  1½ teaspoons grated lemon or lime peel
  ⅓ cup olive or vegetable oil
  ¼ cup chopped fresh basil leaves *or* 2 teaspoons dried basil leaves, crushed*
  1 pound uncooked large shrimp, peeled and deveined
  8 cherry tomatoes
  3 green onions, cut into 2-inch pieces
  8 small mushrooms

In small bowl, blend savory herb with garlic soup mix, lemon juice, lemon peel, oil and basil; add shrimp. Cover and marinate in refrigerator, stirring occasionally, at least 2 hours.

Remove shrimp from marinade, reserving marinade. On 4 skewers, alternately thread shrimp and vegetables. Broil or grill, turning and basting frequently with reserved marinade, until shrimp turn pink.
Makes about 4 servings

*Variation: Substitute 2 teaspoons fennel seeds, crushed.

Menu Suggestion: Serve over hot cooked rice with pineapple slices for dessert.

Meat Loaf with Spinach & Mozzarella

    2 **pounds ground beef**
    1 **envelope Lipton Recipe Secrets Savory Herb with Garlic Soup Mix**
1½ **cups fresh bread crumbs**
    2 **eggs**
    1 **package (10 ounces) frozen whole leaf spinach, thawed and squeezed dry**
    1 **cup shredded mozzarella cheese (about 4 ounces)**
¼ **cup grated Parmesan cheese**

Preheat oven to 350°F.

In medium bowl, thoroughly combine ground beef, savory herb with garlic soup mix, bread crumbs and eggs. Place between two 10×12-inch sheets of waxed paper. Using hands or rolling pin, press into 10×10-inch square. Remove top sheet of waxed paper.

In small bowl, combine spinach with cheeses. Spread over ground beef mixture leaving 1-inch border. Roll, jelly-roll style, removing waxed paper while rolling; seal edge tightly. In 13×9-inch baking or roasting pan, place meat loaf seam side down. Bake 1 hour or until done. Let stand 10 minutes before serving.   Makes about 8 servings

♦ Also terrific with Lipton Recipe Secrets Italian Herb with Tomato, Beefy Onion, Onion or Onion-Mushroom Soup Mix.

Menu Suggestion: Serve with hot buttered noodles, cooked green beans tossed with sliced almonds and a mixed green salad.

Onion-Baked Pork Chops

    1 **envelope Lipton Recipe Secrets Golden Onion Soup Mix**
⅔ **cup dry bread crumbs**
    8 **pork chops, ½ inch thick (about 3 pounds)**
    2 **eggs, well beaten**

Preheat oven to 350°F.

Combine golden onion soup mix with bread crumbs. Dip chops in eggs, then bread crumb mixture, coating well. Place in lightly greased 13×9-inch baking or roasting pan and drizzle, if desired, with melted butter. Bake 1 hour or until chops are done, turning once.   Makes about 8 servings

♦ Also terrific with Lipton Recipe Secrets Onion or Savory Herb with Garlic Soup Mix.

Menu Suggestion: Serve with hot buttered noodles and cooked broccoli.

Country Roasted Chicken Dinner

1 envelope Lipton Recipe Secrets Savory Herb with Garlic Soup Mix
2 tablespoons honey
1 tablespoon water
1 tablespoon butter or margarine, melted
1 roasting chicken (5 to 6 pounds)
3 pounds all-purpose and/or sweet potatoes, cut into chunks

Preheat oven to 350°F.

In small bowl, blend savory herb with garlic soup mix, honey, water and butter.

In 18×12-inch roasting pan, arrange chicken, breast side up; brush with soup mixture. Cover loosely with aluminum foil. Roast 30 minutes; drain. Arrange potatoes around chicken and continue roasting covered, stirring potatoes occasionally, 1 hour or until meat thermometer reaches 175°F and potatoes are tender. *If chicken reaches 175°F before potatoes are tender, remove chicken to serving platter and keep warm. Continue roasting potatoes until tender.* Makes about 8 servings

Note: Insert meat thermometer into thickest part of thigh between breast and thigh; make sure tip does not touch bone.

♦ Also terrific with Lipton Recipe Secrets Golden Herb with Lemon or Golden Onion Soup Mix.

Menu Suggestion: Serve with a mixed green salad, warm biscuits and Lipton Iced Tea.

♦ Quick Crumb Toppings ♦

For a zippy crumb topping for vegetable, chicken or tuna casseroles, combine Lipton Recipe Secrets Onion Soup Mix with fresh bread crumbs, melted butter or margarine and shredded cheese; broil until golden.

♦

Turkey Cottage Pie

¼ cup butter or margarine
¼ cup all-purpose flour
1 envelope Lipton Recipe Secrets Golden Onion or Savory Herb with
    Garlic Soup Mix
2 cups water
2 cups cut-up cooked turkey or chicken
1 package (10 ounces) frozen mixed vegetables, thawed
1¼ cups shredded Swiss or Cheddar cheese (about 5 ounces), divided
5 cups hot mashed potatoes

Preheat oven to 375°F.

In large saucepan, melt butter over medium heat and cook flour, stirring constantly, 5 minutes or until golden. Stir in golden onion soup mix thoroughly blended with water. Bring to a boil over high heat. Reduce heat to low and simmer 15 minutes or until thickened. Stir in turkey, vegetables and 1 cup cheese. Turn into lightly greased 2-quart casserole; top with hot potatoes, then remaining ¼ cup cheese. Bake 30 minutes or until bubbling.

Makes about 8 servings

Menu Suggestion: Serve this all-in-one meal with baked apples or apple pie.

No-Mess Savory Steak

1 chuck or round steak (2 pounds), about 2 inches thick
1 envelope Lipton Recipe Secrets Onion Soup Mix

Preheat oven to 375°F.

On 18×18-inch piece heavy-duty aluminum foil, place steak; sprinkle both sides of steak with onion soup mix. Wrap foil loosely around steak, sealing edges airtight with double fold. Place in 13×9-inch baking or roasting pan and bake 1 hour or until steak is tender. Thicken gravy, if desired, and pour over steak.

Makes about 8 servings

♦ Also terrific with Lipton Recipe Secrets Italian Herb with Tomato or Onion-Mushroom Soup Mix.

Menu Suggestion: Serve with Onion-Roasted Potatoes (page 30) and another favorite vegetable.

Turkey Cottage Pie

Country Herb Roasted Chicken

**1 chicken (2½ to 3 pounds), cut into serving pieces (with or without skin) *or*
    1½ pounds boneless skinless chicken breast halves**
**1 envelope Lipton Recipe Secrets Savory Herb with Garlic or Golden Herb
    with Lemon Soup Mix**
2 tablespoons water
1 tablespoon olive or vegetable oil

Preheat oven to 375°F.

In 13×9-inch baking or roasting pan, arrange chicken. In small bowl,
combine remaining ingredients; brush on chicken.

For *chicken pieces,* bake uncovered 45 minutes or until chicken is done. For
chicken breast halves, bake uncovered 20 minutes or until chicken is done.

Makes about 4 servings

Menu Suggestion: Serve with a lettuce and tomato salad, scalloped
potatoes and cooked green beans.

Home-Style Beef Brisket

1 envelope Lipton Recipe Secrets Onion Soup Mix
¾ cup water
½ cup ketchup
1 teaspoon Lawry's Garlic Powder with Parsley
½ teaspoon ground black pepper
1 brisket of beef (3 pounds)

Preheat oven to 325°F.

In 13×9-inch baking or roasting pan, add onion soup mix blended with
water, ketchup, garlic powder and pepper. Add brisket, turning to coat with
soup mixture. Loosely cover with aluminum foil and roast 3 hours or until
brisket is tender. Thicken gravy, if desired.   Makes about 8 servings

♦ Also terrific with Lipton Recipe Secrets Onion-Mushroom or
   Beefy Onion Soup Mix.

Menu Suggestion: Serve with Onion-Potato Pancakes (page 12) and
applesauce.

Country Herb Roasted Chicken

Southwestern Meat Loaf

   1 envelope Lipton Recipe Secrets Onion Soup Mix
   2 pounds ground beef
   2 cups crushed cornflakes or bran flakes cereal (about 3 ounces)
1½ cups frozen *or* drained canned whole kernel corn
   1 small green bell pepper, chopped
   2 eggs
  ¾ cup water
  ⅓ cup ketchup

Preheat oven to 350°F.

In large bowl, combine all ingredients. In 13×9-inch baking or roasting pan, shape into loaf. Bake 1 hour or until done. Let stand 10 minutes before serving.   Makes about 8 servings

◆ Also terrific with Lipton Recipe Secrets Onion-Mushroom or Beefy Onion Soup Mix.

Menu Suggestion: Serve with salsa, corn bread and Lipton Iced Tea.

Spanish-Style Chicken & Rice

   2 tablespoons olive or vegetable oil
   1 clove garlic, finely chopped
   1 cup uncooked regular rice
   1 envelope Lipton Recipe Secrets Onion Soup Mix
2½ cups hot water
   1 cup frozen peas, partially thawed
  ½ cup chopped red or green bell pepper
   8 green olives, sliced
   1 chicken (2½ to 3 pounds), cut into serving pieces

Preheat oven to 400°F.

In 13×9-inch baking or roasting pan, combine oil with garlic; heat in oven 5 minutes. Stir in uncooked rice until coated with oil. Add onion soup mix blended with hot water; stir in peas, pepper and olives. Press chicken pieces into rice mixture. Bake 35 minutes or until chicken is done and rice is tender. Cover and let stand 10 minutes before serving.

         Makes about 4 servings

Menu Suggestion: Serve with cooked green beans and fresh fruit for dessert.

Southwestern Meat Loaf

Crab-Stuffed Chicken Breasts

1 package (8 ounces) cream cheese, softened
6 ounces frozen crabmeat or imitation crabmeat, thawed and drained
1 envelope Lipton Recipe Secrets Savory Herb with Garlic Soup Mix
6 boneless skinless chicken breast halves (about 1½ pounds)
¼ cup all-purpose flour
2 eggs, beaten
¾ cup plain dry bread crumbs
2 tablespoons olive or vegetable oil
1 tablespoon butter or margarine

Preheat oven to 350°F. Combine cream cheese, crabmeat and savory herb with garlic soup mix; set aside. With knife parallel to cutting board, slice horizontally through each chicken breast, stopping 1 inch from opposite edge; open breasts. Evenly spread each breast with cream cheese mixture. Close each chicken breast, securing open edge with wooden toothpicks.

Dip chicken in flour, then eggs, then bread crumbs, coating well. In 12-inch skillet, heat oil and butter over medium-high heat and cook chicken 10 minutes or until golden, turning once. Transfer chicken to 13×9-inch baking dish and bake uncovered 15 minutes or until chicken is done. Remove toothpicks before serving.   Makes about 6 servings

Menu Suggestion: Serve with a mixed green salad and warm garlic bread.

Souperior Meat Loaf

1 envelope Lipton Recipe Secrets Onion Soup Mix
2 pounds ground beef
1½ cups fresh bread crumbs
2 eggs
¾ cup water
⅓ cup ketchup

Preheat oven to 350°F. In large bowl, combine all ingredients. In 13×9-inch baking or roasting pan, shape into loaf. Bake 1 hour or until done. Let stand 10 minutes before serving.   Makes about 8 servings

♦ Also terrific with Lipton Recipe Secrets Beefy Onion, Onion-Mushroom, Italian Herb with Tomato or Savory Herb with Garlic Soup Mix.

Menu Suggestion: Serve with Mashed Potatoes Florentine (page 32).

Crab-Stuffed Chicken Breasts

Country-Style Turkey Cutlets

  1 envelope Lipton Recipe Secrets Golden Onion or Onion Soup Mix
  ¾ cup plain dry bread crumbs
  ¼ cup grated Parmesan cheese
  1 teaspoon dry mustard
1½ pounds boneless turkey or chicken breasts, pounded ¼ inch thick
  ¼ cup all-purpose flour
  2 eggs, slightly beaten
  ¼ cup butter or margarine, melted

Preheat oven to 350°F. In medium bowl, thoroughly combine golden onion soup mix, bread crumbs, cheese and mustard. Dip turkey in flour, then eggs, then bread crumb mixture, coating well. Place in lightly greased 13×9-inch baking or roasting pan and drizzle with butter. Bake, turning once, 20 minutes or until done.   Makes about 4 servings

Menu Suggestion: Serve with Three Bean Salsa (page 26) and a crisp lettuce wedge with your favorite Wish-Bone Dressing.

Braised Pork Chops with Cabbage & Apple

  ¼ cup all-purpose flour
  ¼ teaspoon salt
  ⅛ teaspoon ground black pepper
  4 pork loin or rib chops, 1 inch thick (about 2 pounds)
  2 tablespoons olive or vegetable oil
1½ pounds savoy or green cabbage, sliced (about 8 cups)
  1 bay leaf (optional)
  1 envelope Lipton Recipe Secrets Onion Soup Mix
  1 cup water
  ½ cup apple juice
  1 medium tart green or red apple, cored and coarsely chopped

Preheat oven to 350°F. Combine flour, salt and pepper; dip pork chops in flour mixture.

In 12-inch skillet, heat oil over medium-high heat and brown chops. Remove chops to 13×9-inch casserole or baking dish; reserve drippings. In reserved drippings, cook cabbage with bay leaf over medium heat, stirring frequently, 5 minutes. Stir in onion soup mix blended with water and apple juice; bring to a boil over high heat. Stir in apple; pour over pork chops. Cover and bake 1 hour or until chops are done. Remove bay leaf.

Makes about 4 servings

Menu Suggestion: Serve with cooked noodles and cookies for dessert.

Chicken Pot Pie

2 tablespoons butter or margarine
**1 pound boneless skinless chicken thighs, cut into 1-inch pieces
    (about 2 cups)***
2 ribs celery, sliced
2 carrots, cut lengthwise in half and sliced
1 medium onion, diced
1 cup frozen cut green beans, thawed
**1 envelope Lipton Recipe Secrets Savory Herb with Garlic or
    Golden Onion Soup Mix**
1 cup milk
1 refrigerated pie crust or pastry for single-crust pie

Preheat oven to 400°F.

In 10-inch skillet, melt butter over medium-high heat and cook chicken, stirring frequently, 8 minutes or until done. With slotted spoon, remove chicken to 9-inch pie plate. Into skillet, stir celery, carrots and onion; cook 8 minutes. Stir in green beans and savory herb with garlic soup mix blended with milk; bring to the boiling point over medium-high heat. Turn into pie plate with chicken; top with crust and seal edges tightly. Pierce crust with fork. Bake 25 minutes or until golden. Let stand 10 minutes before serving.

Makes about 4 servings

*Substitution: Use 2 cups cut-up cooked chicken or turkey and eliminate melting butter and cooking chicken.

Menu Suggestion: Serve with your favorite Lipton Soup and Lipton Iced Tea.

◆ Souper Stuffing ◆

Season bread crumbs with Lipton Recipe Secrets Savory Herb with Garlic Soup Mix for a quick and tasty stuffing, perfect for chicken and turkey.

———————————— ◆ ————————————

From the Grill

Oriental Shrimp & Steak Kabobs

　1 envelope Lipton Recipe Secrets Savory Herb with Garlic or
　　　Onion Soup Mix
¼ cup soy sauce
¼ cup lemon juice
¼ cup olive or vegetable oil
¼ cup honey
½ pound uncooked medium shrimp, peeled and deveined
½ pound boneless sirloin steak, cut into 1-inch cubes
16 cherry tomatoes
　2 cups mushroom caps
　1 medium green bell pepper, cut into chunks

In 13×9-inch glass baking dish, blend savory herb with garlic soup mix, soy sauce, lemon juice, oil and honey; set aside. On skewers, alternately thread shrimp, steak, tomatoes, mushrooms and green pepper. Add prepared skewers to baking dish; turn to coat. Cover and marinate in refrigerator, turning skewers occasionally, at least 2 hours. Remove prepared skewers, reserving marinade. Grill or broil, turning and basting frequently with reserved marinade, until shrimp turn pink and steak is done.

Makes about 8 servings

Menu Suggestion: Serve with corn-on-the-cob, a mixed green salad and grilled garlic bread.

Oriental Shrimp & Steak Kabobs

Marinated Flank Steak

   1 **envelope Lipton Recipe Secrets Onion or Onion-Mushroom Soup Mix**
½ **cup water**
½ **cup dry red wine**
¼ **cup olive or vegetable oil**
   1 **tablespoon finely chopped parsley**
   1 **flank steak (2 pounds)**

In large nonaluminum baking dish, thoroughly blend all ingredients except steak; add steak and turn to coat. Cover and marinate steak in refrigerator, turning occasionally, at least 4 hours. Remove steak, reserving marinade.

Grill or broil steak until done, turning once. Meanwhile, in small saucepan, bring remaining marinade to a boil over high heat. Reduce heat to low and simmer 5 minutes. If necessary, skim fat from marinade. Serve hot marinade with steak.   Makes about 8 servings

Menu Suggestion: Serve with Grilled Potatoes (page 69) and your favorite vegetable.

◆ Hot Off the Grill ◆

Cleanup is easier if you coat the grill rack with no stick cooking spray before barbecuing.

If you use a charcoal grill, remember that a fire is ready for cooking when the coals are covered with gray ash—about 20 to 30 minutes after lighting.

Toss damp hickory chunks, outer onion layers or garlic halves on hot coals to flavor meats, poultry and fish. Grated orange and lemon peel also add a light touch to fruits and vegetables.

"Kabob-it" by skewering chunks of fresh melon, pineapple, apples, pears or peaches and grill for a toasted fruit salad. Sprinkle with coconut for grilled "ambrosia."

◆

Lipton Onion Butter

1 envelope Lipton Recipe Secrets Onion Soup Mix
1 container (8 ounces) whipped butter or soft margarine *or* ½ pound butter
or margarine, softened

Thoroughly blend onion soup mix with butter. Store covered in refrigerator.
Makes about 1¼ cups onion butter

Serving Suggestions:

ONION-BUTTERED GRILLED VEGETABLES: Brush Lipton Onion Butter
on sliced red onion, eggplant, tomatoes or corn-on-the-cob; grill or broil
until vegetables are tender.

ONION-BUTTERED BREAD: Spread Lipton Onion Butter between slices of
French or Italian bread; wrap in aluminum foil and grill until butter is
melted.

ONION-BUTTERED SANDWICHES: Spread softened Lipton Onion Butter
on bread slices when making sandwiches. Especially good with roast beef,
cheese, lettuce and tomatoes.

ONION-BUTTERED POPCORN: Toss 2½ quarts popped popcorn with
½ cup melted Lipton Onion Butter.

Stuffed Burgers Italiano

1 envelope Lipton Recipe Secrets Italian Herb with Tomato Soup Mix
1½ pounds ground beef
3 ounces mozzarella cheese, cut into 6 cubes

Combine Italian herb with tomato soup mix and ground beef; shape into
6 (6-inch) patties. Place 1 cheese cube in center of each patty. Bring sides
over to enclose cheese; shape into burger. Grill or broil until done.
Makes 6 servings

♦ Also terrific with Lipton Recipe Secrets Savory Herb with Garlic, Onion,
Onion-Mushroom or Beefy Onion Soup Mix.

Menu Suggestion: Serve on sesame seed rolls with corn-on-the-cob and a
sliced tomato and cucumber salad.

Grilled Pasta Salad

   4 medium zucchini and/or yellow squash, sliced
   1 medium Spanish onion, halved and cut into large chunks
   1 envelope Lipton Recipe Secrets Savory Herb with Garlic Soup Mix
   ¼ cup olive or vegetable oil
   8 ounces penne, rotini or ziti pasta, cooked and drained
   ¾ cup diced roasted red peppers
   ¼ cup red wine vinegar, apple cider vinegar or white vinegar

On heavy-duty aluminum foil or on broiler pan, arrange zucchini and onion. Brush with savory herb with garlic soup mix blended with oil. Grill or broil 5 minutes or until golden brown and crisp-tender.

In large bowl, toss cooked pasta, vegetables, roasted peppers and vinegar. Serve warm or at room temperature.

Makes about 4 main-dish or 8 side-dish servings

♦ Also terrific with Lipton Recipe Secrets Italian Herb with Tomato or Golden Onion Soup Mix.

Menu Suggestion: Serve with hot crusty bread and a spinach salad.

Grilled Greek-Style Chicken

   1 container (8 ounces) plain yogurt
   ¼ cup chopped fresh mint or parsley leaves
   1 envelope Lipton Recipe Secrets Savory Herb with Garlic Soup Mix
   1 pound boneless skinless chicken breast halves

In small shallow glass baking dish, blend yogurt, mint and savory herb with garlic soup mix. Add chicken and turn to coat. Cover and marinate in refrigerator, turning chicken occasionally, at least 2 hours. Remove chicken, reserving marinade. Grill or broil chicken, turning once and basting with reserved marinade, until chicken is done.   Makes about 4 servings

Menu Suggestion: Serve with Oven-Roasted Vegetables (page 22) and rice pilaf.

Grilled Pasta Salad

Fresco Marinated Chicken

1 envelope Lipton Recipe Secrets Savory Herb with Garlic Soup Mix
½ cup water
2 tablespoons olive or vegetable oil
1 teaspoon lemon juice or vinegar
1 pound boneless skinless chicken breast halves

In large nonaluminum baking dish, blend savory herb with garlic soup mix, water, oil and lemon juice; add chicken and turn to coat. Cover and marinate in refrigerator at least 1 hour or overnight.

On broiler pan or grill lined with heavy-duty aluminum foil, lightly sprayed with no stick cooking spray, arrange chicken; pour ½ of the marinade over chicken. Grill or broil, turning once and pouring remaining marinade over chicken, until done.   Makes about 4 servings

◆ Also terrific with Lipton Recipe Secrets Golden Onion or Golden Herb with Lemon Soup Mix.

Menu Suggestion: Serve with a tomato salad and cooked rice tossed with mushrooms and sliced green onions.

Grilled Reuben Burgers

1 envelope Lipton Recipe Secrets Onion-Mushroom Soup Mix
1½ pounds ground beef
½ cup water
½ cup shredded Swiss cheese (about 2 ounces)
1 tablespoon crisp-cooked crumbled bacon or bacon bits
½ teaspoon caraway seeds (optional)

In large bowl, combine all ingredients; shape into 6 patties. Grill or broil until done. Top, if desired, with heated sauerkraut and additional bacon.
                    Makes 6 servings

◆ Also terrific with Lipton Recipe Secrets Onion or Beefy Onion Soup Mix.

Menu Suggestion: Serve with coleslaw, pickles and Lipton Iced Tea.

Fresco Marinated Chicken

Summer Vegetable & Fish Bundles

   4 fish fillets (about 1 pound)
   1 pound thinly sliced vegetables*
   1 envelope Lipton Recipe Secrets Savory Herb with Garlic or
        Golden Onion Soup Mix
 ½ cup water

On two 18×18-inch pieces heavy-duty aluminum foil, divide fish equally; top with vegetables. Evenly pour savory herb with garlic soup mix blended with water over fish. Wrap foil loosely around fillets and vegetables, sealing edges airtight with double fold. Grill or broil seam-side-up 15 minutes or until fish flakes.   Makes about 4 servings

*Use any combination of the following: thinly sliced mushrooms, zucchini, yellow squash or tomatoes.

Menu Suggestion: Serve over hot cooked rice with Lipton Iced Tea mixed with a splash of cranberry juice cocktail.

Tempting Taco Burgers

   1 envelope Lipton Recipe Secrets Onion-Mushroom Soup Mix
   1 pound ground beef
 ½ cup chopped tomato
 ¼ cup finely chopped green bell pepper
 ¼ cup water
   1 teaspoon chili powder

In large bowl, combine all ingredients; shape into 4 patties. Grill or broil until done. Serve, if desired, on hamburger rolls and top with shredded lettuce and shredded Cheddar cheese.   Makes about 4 servings

♦ Also terrific with Lipton Recipe Secrets Onion or Beefy Onion Soup Mix.

Menu Suggestion: Serve with salsa and tortilla chips.

Sweet 'n Spicy Onion Glaze

1 envelope Lipton Recipe Secrets Onion Soup Mix
1 jar (20 ounces) apricot preserves
1 cup (8 ounces) Wish-Bone Sweet 'n Spicy French Dressing

In small bowl, blend all ingredients. Use as a glaze for chicken, spareribs, kabobs, hamburgers or frankfurters. Brush on during last half of cooking. Glaze can be stored covered in refrigerator up to 2 weeks.

Makes about 2½ cups glaze

Note: Recipe can be doubled.

♦ Also terrific with Wish-Bone Lite Sweet 'n Spicy French, Russian or Lite Russian Dressing.

Menu Suggestion: Serve cooked, glazed meat or poultry with potato salad and coleslaw.

Lipton Onion Burgers

1 envelope Lipton Recipe Secrets Onion Soup Mix
2 pounds ground beef
½ cup water

In large bowl, combine all ingredients; shape into 8 patties. Grill or broil until done.

Makes about 8 servings

♦ Also terrific with Lipton Recipe Secrets Beefy Onion, Onion-Mushroom or Italian Herb with Tomato Soup Mix.

Menu Suggestion: Serve with lettuce, tomato, pickles and potato salad.

Honey-Lime Pork Chops

**1 envelope Lipton Recipe Secrets Savory Herb with Garlic or
    Onion Soup Mix**
3 tablespoons soy sauce
2 tablespoons honey
2 tablespoons lime juice
1 teaspoon grated fresh ginger *or* ¼ teaspoon ground ginger (optional)
4 boneless pork chops, 1½ inches thick (about 1 pound)

In 13×9-inch glass baking dish, blend all ingredients except pork chops. Add chops and turn to coat. Cover and marinate in refrigerator, turning chops occasionally, at least 2 hours. Remove chops, reserving marinade. Grill or broil chops, turning once and basting with reserved marinade, until done.

Makes about 4 servings

Menu Suggestion: Serve with baked potatoes topped with plain yogurt or sour cream and your favorite vegetable.

Grilled Potatoes

4 medium baking potatoes, diced
½ cup Lipton Onion Butter (see page 61)
Chopped parsley

On four 18×10-inch pieces heavy-duty aluminum foil, divide potatoes equally; top each with 2 tablespoons Lipton Onion Butter and sprinkle with parsley. Wrap foil loosely around potatoes, sealing edges airtight with double fold. Grill 30 minutes or until tender.   Makes 4 servings

Menu Suggestion: Serve with Marinated Flank Steak (page 60) and Lipton Iced Tea.

Top-of-Stove Entrées

No-Peek Skillet Chicken

    2 tablespoons olive or vegetable oil
    1 chicken (2½ to 3 pounds), cut into serving pieces (with or without skin)
    1 can (14½ ounces) whole peeled tomatoes, undrained and chopped
    ½ cup sliced fresh *or* drained canned mushrooms
    1 clove garlic, minced
    1 envelope Lipton Recipe Secrets Onion Soup Mix
      Hot cooked noodles

In 12-inch skillet, heat oil over medium-high heat and brown chicken; drain.
Stir in tomatoes, mushrooms and garlic combined with onion soup mix.
Reduce heat to low and simmer covered 45 minutes or until chicken is done.
Serve over hot noodles and sprinkle, if desired, with chopped fresh parsley.

Makes about 6 servings

♦ Also terrific with Lipton Recipe Secrets Italian Herb with Tomato, Savory
  Herb with Garlic, Golden Herb with Lemon or Beefy Onion Soup Mix.

Menu Suggestion: Serve with a mixed green salad and Lipton Iced Tea.

No-Peek Skillet Chicken

Hearty Meatless Chili

    1 envelope Lipton Recipe Secrets Onion or Onion-Mushroom Soup Mix
    4 cups water
    1 can (16 ounces) chick-peas or garbanzo beans, rinsed and drained
    1 can (16 ounces) red kidney beans, rinsed and drained
    1 can (14½ ounces) whole peeled tomatoes, undrained and chopped
    1 cup lentils, rinsed and drained
    1 large rib celery, coarsely chopped
    1 tablespoon chili powder
    2 teaspoons ground cumin (optional)
    1 medium clove garlic, finely chopped

In 4-quart saucepan or stockpot, combine all ingredients. Bring to a boil over high heat. Reduce heat to low and simmer covered, stirring occasionally, 20 minutes or until lentils are almost tender. Remove cover and simmer, stirring occasionally, an additional 20 minutes or until liquid is almost absorbed and lentils are tender.   Makes about 4 (2-cup) servings

Note: For spicier chili, add ¼ teaspoon crushed red pepper flakes.

Serving Suggestion: Serve over hot cooked brown or white rice and top with shredded Cheddar cheese.

Santa Fe Stir Fry

    1 envelope Lipton Recipe Secrets Onion Soup Mix
    ¼ cup olive or vegetable oil
    ¼ cup water
    1 tablespoon lime juice (optional)
    ½ teaspoon Lawry's Garlic Powder with Parsley
    1 pound boneless skinless chicken breasts, cut into thin strips
    2 cups frozen assorted vegetables, partially thawed and drained
      Hot cooked rice

In 12-inch skillet, blend onion soup mix, oil, water, lime juice and garlic powder; let stand 5 minutes. Bring to a boil over high heat; stir in chicken and vegetables. Cook uncovered, stirring frequently, 5 minutes or until chicken is done. Serve over hot rice. Garnish, if desired, with chopped fresh parsley and lime slices.   Makes about 4 servings

♦ Also terrific with Lipton Recipe Secrets Onion-Mushroom or Savory Herb with Garlic Soup Mix.

Menu Suggestion: Serve with Lipton Iced Tea and frozen yogurt for dessert.

Savory Stuffed Beef Rollatini

      2 tablespoons olive or vegetable oil, divided
      1 large onion, chopped
      2 cups fresh bread crumbs
      ⅓ cup grated Parmesan cheese
      ¼ cup chopped fresh parsley
      6 beef top round steaks or braciola, each ¼ inch thick (about 1½ pounds)
      1 envelope Lipton Recipe Secrets Italian Herb with Tomato or
            Savory Herb with Garlic Soup Mix
 1½ cups water

In 10-inch skillet, heat 1 tablespoon oil over medium heat and cook onion,
stirring occasionally, 2 minutes. Remove from heat; stir in bread crumbs,
cheese and parsley. Place ½ cup bread crumb mixture on each piece of meat.
Roll, starting at longer end, jelly-roll style; secure with wooden toothpicks.
In same skillet, heat remaining 1 tablespoon oil over medium-high heat and
brown meat; drain. Add Italian herb with tomato soup mix blended with
water. Bring to a boil over high heat. Reduce heat to low and simmer
covered 1 hour or until beef is tender. Remove toothpicks before serving.

Makes about 6 servings

Menu Suggestion: Serve with hot cooked pasta and warm crusty bread.

Country-Style Pot Roast

      1 boneless pot roast (3 to 3½ pounds), rump, chuck or round
      1 envelope Lipton Recipe Secrets Onion-Mushroom Soup Mix
 2½ cups water, divided
      4 potatoes, cut into 1-inch pieces
      4 carrots, thinly sliced
      2 to 4 tablespoons all-purpose flour

In 5-quart Dutch oven or heavy saucepot, brown roast over medium-high
heat. Add onion-mushroom soup mix blended with 2 cups water. Reduce
heat to low and simmer covered, turning occasionally, 2 hours. Add
vegetables and cook an additional 30 minutes or until vegetables and roast
are tender; remove roast and vegetables. Blend remaining ½ cup water with
flour; stir into Dutch oven. Bring to a boil over high heat. Reduce heat to
low and simmer, stirring constantly, until thickened, about 5 minutes.

Makes about 6 servings

♦ Also terrific with Lipton Recipe Secrets Onion, Beefy Onion or Italian
   Herb with Tomato Soup Mix.

Menu Suggestion: Serve with warm rolls and apple pie for dessert.

Country French Chicken Breasts

1 tablespoon butter or margarine
1 pound boneless skinless chicken breast halves
1 envelope Lipton Recipe Secrets Savory Herb with Garlic or
    Golden Onion Soup Mix
1 cup water
1 tablespoon lemon juice
4 lemon slices (optional)
   Hot cooked rice

In 12-inch skillet, melt butter over medium-high heat and brown chicken. Stir in savory herb with garlic soup mix blended with water and lemon juice; arrange lemon slices on chicken. Reduce heat to low and simmer covered 10 minutes or until sauce is slightly thickened and chicken is done. To serve, arrange chicken over rice and spoon sauce over chicken.

Makes about 4 servings

Menu Suggestion: Serve with your favorite Lipton Soup.

Pork Chops Piquante

2 teaspoons olive or vegetable oil, divided
4 pork chops, ¾ inch thick
1 medium onion, thinly sliced
1½ teaspoons ketchup
½ cup dry white wine
1 envelope Lipton Recipe Secrets Savory Herb with Garlic Soup Mix
1¼ cups water
2 tablespoons finely sliced sweet gherkin pickles

In 12-inch skillet, heat 1 teaspoon oil over medium-high heat and brown chops; remove and set aside. In same skillet, heat remaining 1 teaspoon oil over medium heat and brown onion. Add ketchup and cook over medium heat, stirring frequently, 1 minute. Add wine and boil over high heat 1 minute. Stir in savory herb with garlic soup mix blended with water. Bring to a boil over high heat; reduce heat to low. Return pork chops to skillet and simmer covered 10 minutes. Add pickles and continue simmering 5 minutes or until pork is done.

Makes about 4 servings

Menu Suggestion: Serve with baked potatoes and applesauce.

Country French Chicken Breasts

Frittata with Artichokes

    1 envelope Lipton Recipe Secrets Savory Herb with Garlic Soup Mix
    8 eggs
    ¾ cup milk
    1 teaspoon butter or margarine
    1 cup diced and drained canned artichoke hearts (about 4 ounces)

In medium bowl, blend savory herb with garlic soup mix, eggs and milk; set aside. In omelet pan or 8-inch skillet, melt butter over low heat and cook egg mixture, lifting set edges with spatula and tilting pan to allow uncooked mixture to flow to bottom. When bottom is set, top with artichokes. Reduce heat to low and simmer covered 3 minutes or until eggs are set.

Makes about 4 servings

♦ Also terrific with Lipton Recipe Secrets Golden Herb with Lemon or Golden Onion Soup Mix.

Menu Suggestion: Serve with Lipton Noodle Soup and a mixed green salad.

Chicken Breasts with Savory Mustard Herb Sauce

    2 tablespoons olive or vegetable oil, divided
    1 pound boneless skinless chicken breast halves
    1 medium zucchini, sliced
 1½ cups sliced fresh *or* drained canned mushrooms
    1 envelope Lipton Recipe Secrets Savory Herb with Garlic or
        Golden Onion Soup Mix
    ¾ cup water
    2 teaspoons Dijon-style, country Dijon-style or brown prepared mustard

In 12-inch skillet, heat 1 tablespoon oil over medium-high heat and cook chicken 5 minutes or until almost done, turning once; remove and keep warm. In same skillet, heat remaining 1 tablespoon oil over medium heat and cook zucchini and mushrooms, stirring frequently, 3 minutes. Return chicken to skillet; stir in savory herb with garlic soup mix blended with water and mustard. Bring to a boil over high heat. Reduce heat to low and simmer covered 5 minutes or until chicken is done. To serve, arrange chicken on serving platter and top with sauce mixture.

Makes about 4 servings

Menu Suggestion: Serve with cooked noodles and a fresh fruit salad.

Frittata with Artichokes

"Messy Hanks"

1 envelope Lipton Recipe Secrets Onion Soup Mix
¾ cup chili sauce
¼ cup grape jelly
2 tablespoons water
1 pound ground beef
1 medium green bell pepper, finely chopped
6 hoagie or hamburger rolls or English muffins

In small bowl, combine onion soup mix, chili sauce, grape jelly and water.
In 10-inch skillet, brown ground beef with green pepper over medium-high
heat; drain. Stir in soup mixture. Bring to a boil over high heat. Reduce heat
to low and simmer, stirring occasionally, 5 minutes or until slightly
thickened. Serve on rolls.   Makes about 6 servings

♦ Also terrific with Lipton Recipe Secrets Beefy Onion, Onion-Mushroom
  or Savory Herb with Garlic Soup Mix.

Menu Suggestion: Serve with a lettuce and tomato salad, tortilla chips
and ice cream with a choice of toppings.

Chicken & Artichoke Sauté

2 tablespoons olive or vegetable oil, divided
1 chicken (2½ to 3 pounds), quartered
1 medium onion, chopped
1 envelope Lipton Recipe Secrets Savory Herb with Garlic Soup Mix
1½ cups water
1 can (15 ounces) artichoke hearts, drained

In 12-inch skillet, heat 1½ tablespoons oil over medium-high heat and brown
chicken. Remove chicken and drain. Into same skillet, add remaining
½ tablespoon oil and cook onion 2 minutes. Stir in savory herb with garlic
soup mix blended with water; bring to a boil over high heat. Return chicken
to skillet; add artichokes. Reduce heat to low and simmer covered
20 minutes or until chicken is done.   Makes about 4 servings

♦ Also terrific with Lipton Recipe Secrets Italian Herb with Tomato or
  Golden Herb with Lemon Soup Mix.

Menu Suggestion: Serve over hot cooked rice, couscous or noodles.

"Messy Hanks"

Stove-Top Barbecue Beef

1 tablespoon olive or vegetable oil
2 pounds boneless beef chuck, cut into 2-inch pieces
2 carrots, diced
1 large green bell pepper, diced
2 to 3 tablespoons chili powder
1 envelope Lipton Recipe Secrets Onion Soup Mix
1 cup water
1 can (8 ounces) tomato sauce
2 tablespoons firmly packed brown sugar
2 tablespoons cider vinegar
½ teaspoon hot pepper sauce*
8 round rolls or hamburger buns

In 5-quart Dutch oven or heavy saucepot, heat oil over medium-high heat and brown beef in two batches. Remove and set aside; reserve drippings. Add carrots, green pepper and chili powder to reserved drippings and cook over medium heat, stirring frequently, 2 minutes. Stir in onion soup mix blended with water, tomato sauce, brown sugar and cider vinegar. Return beef to Dutch oven. Bring to a boil over high heat. Reduce heat to low and simmer covered, stirring occasionally, 2½ hours or until meat is very tender. Stir in hot pepper sauce. Using two forks, shred beef. Reheat meat mixture if necessary. Serve on rolls.   Makes about 8 servings

*Use more, if desired.

Menu Suggestion: Serve with Warm Potato Salad (page 28) and cut-up fresh fruit or brownies for dessert.

Chicken with Golden Caper Sauce

1 pound boneless skinless chicken breast halves
1 egg, beaten
   All-purpose flour
2 tablespoons butter or margarine
1 tablespoon olive or vegetable oil
1 small onion, finely chopped
1 envelope Lipton Recipe Secrets Golden Herb with Lemon or
      Savory Herb with Garlic Soup Mix
1 cup water
1 teaspoon Dijon-style, country Dijon-style or brown prepared mustard
1 tablespoon capers, drained and chopped

Dip chicken in egg, then flour. In 12-inch skillet, heat butter and oil over medium-high heat and brown chicken 8 minutes or until chicken is done, turning once. (Butter will begin to brown.) Remove chicken to serving dish and keep warm.

In same skillet, cook onion over medium heat 2 minutes or until soft. Add golden herb with lemon soup mix blended with water and mustard. Bring to a boil over high heat. Reduce heat to low and simmer uncovered, stirring occasionally, 4 minutes. Stir in capers and simmer 1 minute. To serve, pour sauce over chicken. Garnish, if desired, with chopped fresh parsley.

Makes about 4 servings

Menu Suggestion: Serve with rice pilaf and a mixed green salad.

Hearty Beef Carbonnade

4 slices bacon
2 pounds boneless beef chuck, cut into 1-inch cubes
1 large clove garlic, finely chopped
1 bay leaf (optional)
1 envelope Lipton Recipe Secrets Onion Soup Mix
1 can (12 ounces) beer *or* 1½ cups water
1 cup water
1 tablespoon red wine vinegar
1 tablespoon finely chopped fresh parsley (optional)

In 6-quart Dutch oven or heavy saucepot, cook bacon over medium-high heat; remove, crumble and set aside. Reserve 1 tablespoon drippings. Add ½ of the beef to reserved drippings and brown over medium-high heat; remove beef and set aside. Repeat with remaining beef. Remove beef and set aside. Add garlic to drippings and cook over medium heat, stirring frequently, 1 minute. Return beef to Dutch oven. Add bay leaf and onion soup mix blended with beer and 1 cup water. Bring to a boil over high heat. Reduce heat to low and simmer covered, stirring occasionally, 1 hour 15 minutes or until beef is tender. Remove bay leaf. Skim fat, if necessary. Stir in vinegar and parsley and garnish with bacon.

Makes about 8 servings

Menu Suggestion: Serve with hot cooked rice and broccoli.

Garlic Shrimp with Wilted Spinach

2 teaspoons olive or vegetable oil
¼ cup diagonally sliced green onions
2 tablespoons sherry or dry white wine (optional)
1 envelope Lipton Recipe Secrets Savory Herb with Garlic Soup Mix
1 cup water
1 pound uncooked medium shrimp, peeled and deveined
1 large tomato, diced
2 cups fresh trimmed spinach leaves (about 4 ounces)
¼ cup chopped unsalted cashews (optional)

In 12-inch skillet, heat oil over medium heat and cook green onions, stirring occasionally, 2 minutes or until slightly soft. Add sherry and bring to a boil over high heat, stirring frequently. Stir in savory herb with garlic soup mix blended with water. Bring to a boil over high heat. Reduce heat to low and simmer 2 minutes or until sauce is thickened. Stir in shrimp, tomato, spinach and cashews. Simmer, stirring occasionally, 2 minutes or until shrimp turn pink.   Makes about 4 servings

♦ Also terrific with Lipton Recipe Secrets Golden Herb with Lemon or Golden Onion Soup Mix.

Menu Suggestion: Serve with hot cooked rice and fresh fruit for dessert.

♦ Leftover Magic ♦

Collect, store and freeze celery leaves, parsley stems, asparagus, broccoli stalks, and other vegetable trimmings in reclosable storage bags. Add them to soups and stews for added flavor and nutrients—even those you make with Lipton Recipe Secrets Soup Mixes.

Grate bits of leftover cheese, put in a plastic bag and freeze. Use to top casseroles, sprinkle on vegetables or salads, or mix into sandwich fillings.

♦

Garlic Shrimp with Wilted Spinach

Country Chicken Stew with Dumplings

  1 tablespoon olive or vegetable oil
  1 chicken (3 to 3½ pounds), cut into serving pieces (with or without skin)
  4 large carrots, cut into 2-inch pieces
  3 ribs celery, cut into 1-inch pieces
  1 large onion, cut into 1-inch wedges
  1 envelope Lipton Recipe Secrets Savory Herb with Garlic Soup Mix
1½ cups water
 ½ cup apple juice
   Parsley Dumplings, optional (recipe follows)

In 6-quart Dutch oven or heavy saucepot, heat oil over medium-high heat and brown ½ of the chicken; remove and set aside. Repeat with remaining chicken. Return chicken to Dutch oven. Stir in carrots, celery, onion and savory herb with garlic soup mix blended with water and apple juice. Bring to a boil over high heat. Reduce heat to low and simmer covered 25 minutes or until chicken is done and vegetables are tender.

Meanwhile, prepare Parsley Dumplings. Drop 12 rounded tablespoonfuls of batter into simmering broth around chicken. Continue simmering covered 10 minutes or until toothpick inserted in center of dumpling comes out clean. Season stew, if desired, with salt and pepper.

Makes about 6 servings

PARSLEY DUMPLINGS: In medium bowl, combine 1⅓ cups all-purpose flour, 2 teaspoons baking powder, 1 tablespoon chopped fresh parsley and ½ teaspoon salt; set aside. In measuring cup, blend ⅔ cup milk, 2 tablespoons melted butter or margarine and 1 egg. Stir milk mixture into flour mixture just until blended.

Variation: Add 1 pound quartered red potatoes to stew with carrots; eliminate dumplings.

♦ Also terrific with Lipton Recipe Secrets Golden Onion or Golden Herb with Lemon Soup Mix.

Menu Suggestion: Serve this as a meal-in-one!

Country Chicken Stew with Dumplings

Crunchy Cutlets with Corn Salsa

    1 egg, beaten
    1 tablespoon plus 1 cup water, divided
    1 pound boneless skinless chicken breast halves, pounded to ¼-inch
        thickness
  ½ cup yellow cornmeal
  ½ teaspoon salt
    2 tablespoons plus 1½ teaspoons olive or vegetable oil, divided
    2 green onions, sliced (about ¾ cup)
    1 large red bell pepper, diced (about 1 cup)
    1 package (10 ounces) frozen whole kernel corn, partially thawed
    1 envelope Lipton Recipe Secrets Golden Onion or Golden Herb with
        Lemon Soup Mix
    1 to 2 tablespoons chopped fresh cilantro (optional)

In small bowl, beat egg with 1 tablespoon water. Dip chicken in egg, then cornmeal combined with salt. In 12-inch skillet, heat 1 tablespoon oil over medium-high heat and cook ½ of the chicken 4 minutes or until done, turning once. Remove chicken to platter; keep warm. Repeat with remaining chicken and 1 tablespoon oil.

Wipe out skillet. Heat remaining 1½ teaspoons oil in skillet over medium heat and cook green onions and red pepper 1 minute, stirring constantly. Add corn and golden onion soup mix blended with remaining 1 cup water. Bring to a boil over high heat. Reduce heat to low and simmer 7 minutes or until vegetables are tender and liquid is thickened. Stir in cilantro. To serve, spoon corn salsa over chicken.   Makes about 4 servings

Menu Suggestion: Serve with a tomato salad and pineapple slices for dessert.

Fish Fillets with Ragoût Sauce

1½ teaspoons butter or margarine
    3 large red, green and/or yellow bell peppers, cut into very thin strips
        (about 3 cups)
    3 tablespoons dry white wine or water
    1 envelope Lipton Recipe Secrets Savory Herb with Garlic or
        Golden Onion Soup Mix
1½ cups water
    1 tablespoon lemon juice
    1 pound fish fillets

In 12-inch skillet, melt butter over medium heat and cook peppers, stirring occasionally, 5 minutes or until softened. Remove ½ of the peppers; reserve. Add wine to skillet and bring to a boil over high heat, stirring frequently. Stir in savory herb with garlic soup mix blended with water and lemon juice. Bring to a boil over high heat. Reduce heat to low and continue simmering 10 minutes or until sauce is slightly thickened.

Meanwhile, top fish with equal portions of reserved peppers; roll up and secure with wooden toothpicks. Arrange fish in skillet and simmer covered 8 minutes or until fish flakes. Remove toothpicks before serving.

Makes about 4 servings

Menu Suggestion: Serve with rice pilaf and hot crusty bread.

Hearty Bistro Chicken

    2 tablespoons olive or vegetable oil
    1 chicken (2½ to 3 pounds), cut into serving pieces (with or without skin)
    2 ears fresh or frozen corn, cut into 1½-inch pieces
    1 package (8 ounces) frozen snap peas *or* 1 package (10 ounces) frozen
        green beans
    1 cup frozen sliced or baby carrots
    1 envelope Lipton Recipe Secrets Onion Soup Mix
    2 cups water
    ¼ cup sherry (optional)
    2 tablespoons Dijon-style, country Dijon-style or brown prepared mustard
    2 tablespoons all-purpose flour
    1 container (8 ounces) sour cream

In 12-inch skillet, heat oil over medium-high heat and brown chicken; drain. Add corn, peas and carrots; then add onion soup mix blended with water, sherry and mustard. Bring to a boil over high heat. Reduce heat to low and simmer covered 20 minutes or until chicken is done.

Remove chicken and vegetables to serving platter and keep warm; reserve liquid. Boil reserved liquid over high heat 10 minutes. Remove from heat and stir in flour blended with sour cream; return to heat. Bring just to the boiling point over medium-high heat. Reduce heat to low and simmer, stirring constantly, until sauce is thickened, about 3 minutes. To serve, pour sauce over chicken and vegetables.

Makes about 4 servings

♦ Also terrific with Lipton Recipe Secrets Golden Herb with Lemon, Golden Onion or Savory Herb with Garlic Soup Mix.

Menu Suggestion: Serve with a mixed green salad and fresh fruit for dessert.

Steaks with Peppers

    2 tablespoons olive or vegetable oil
1½ pounds boneless beef chuck steaks, ½ inch thick (about 4 to 5)
    2 medium red, green and/or yellow bell peppers, cut into thin strips
    1 clove garlic, finely chopped (optional)
    1 medium tomato, coarsely chopped
    1 envelope Lipton Recipe Secrets Onion or Onion-Mushroom Soup Mix
    1 cup water

In 12-inch skillet, heat oil over medium-high heat and brown steaks. Remove steaks. Add peppers and garlic to skillet; cook over medium heat 5 minutes or until peppers are crisp-tender. Stir in tomato, then onion soup mix blended with water; bring to a boil over high heat. Reduce heat to low. Return steaks to skillet and simmer uncovered, stirring sauce occasionally, 25 minutes or until steaks and vegetables are tender.

Makes about 4 servings

Menu Suggestion: Serve with steak fries or baked potatoes.

Savory Chicken Breasts Provençal

    1 tablespoon olive or vegetable oil
    2 whole chicken breasts (about 1 pound *each*), split
¼ cup dry white wine or water
    1 large tomato, chopped
    1 envelope Lipton Recipe Secrets Savory Herb with Garlic Soup Mix
¾ cup water
    2 tablespoons sliced pitted ripe olives
    1 tablespoon chopped fresh parsley (optional)

In 12-inch skillet, heat oil over medium-high heat and brown chicken 10 minutes, turning once; drain. Remove chicken and keep warm. Add wine to skillet and boil over high heat 2 minutes, stirring brown bits from bottom of skillet. Stir in tomato and savory herb with garlic soup mix blended with water. Bring to a boil over high heat. Reduce heat to low and return chicken to skillet. Simmer covered 20 minutes or until chicken is done. Top with olives and parsley.

Makes about 4 servings

♦ Also terrific with Lipton Recipe Secrets Golden Onion or Golden Herb with Lemon Soup Mix.

Menu Suggestion: Serve with hot buttered rice or noodles.

Savory Chicken with Mushrooms & Spinach

2 tablespoons olive or vegetable oil, divided
1 pound boneless skinless chicken breast halves, pounded thin
8 ounces fresh spinach leaves, rinsed and drained*
1½ cups sliced fresh *or* drained canned mushrooms
1 envelope Lipton Recipe Secrets Savory Herb with Garlic Soup Mix
1 cup water

In 12-inch skillet, heat 1 tablespoon oil over medium-high heat and cook chicken until done; remove and keep warm.

In same skillet, heat remaining 1 tablespoon oil over medium heat and cook spinach and mushrooms, stirring frequently, 3 minutes. Stir in savory herb with garlic soup mix blended with water. Bring to a boil over high heat; continue boiling, stirring occasionally, 1 minute or until sauce is thickened. To serve, arrange chicken over vegetable mixture.

Makes about 4 servings

*Substitution: Use 1 package (10 ounces) frozen leaf spinach, thawed and squeezed dry.

◆ Also terrific with Lipton Recipe Secrets Golden Herb with Lemon or Golden Onion Soup Mix.

Menu Suggestion: Serve with Onion-Roasted Potatoes (page 30) and warm dinner rolls.

◆ Simple Tricks with Lipton Recipe Secrets Soup Mixes ◆

Substitute 1 envelope Lipton Recipe Secrets Golden Onion Soup Mix blended with 1½ to 2 cups water for 1½ to 2 cups chicken broth in your recipes. You'll get more flavor... plus a bonus of tender onion pieces.

Substitute 1 envelope Lipton Recipe Secrets Onion, Onion-Mushroom or Beefy Onion Soup Mix blended with 2 cups water for every 2 cups beef broth needed in a recipe.

Combine Lipton Recipe Secrets Onion Soup Mix with sour cream and use as a topping for nachos, tacos or baked potatoes.

⸻⸻⸻ ◆ ⸻⸻⸻

Savory Chicken with Mushrooms & Spinach

Southwestern Beef Stew

  1 tablespoon plus 1 teaspoon olive or vegetable oil, divided
1½ pounds boneless beef chuck, cut into 1-inch cubes
  1 can (4 ounces) chopped green chilies, drained
  2 large cloves garlic, finely chopped
  1 teaspoon ground cumin (optional)
  1 can (14 to 16 ounces) whole or plum tomatoes, undrained and chopped
  1 envelope Lipton Recipe Secrets Onion or Beefy Onion Soup Mix
  1 cup water
  1 package (10 ounces) frozen cut okra or green beans, thawed
  1 large red or green bell pepper, cut into 1-inch pieces
  4 frozen half-ears corn-on-the-cob, thawed and each cut into 3 round pieces
  2 tablespoons chopped fresh cilantro (optional)

In 5-quart Dutch oven or heavy saucepot, heat 1 tablespoon oil over medium-high heat and brown ½ of the beef; remove and set aside. Repeat with remaining beef; remove and set aside. In same Dutch oven, heat remaining 1 teaspoon oil over medium heat and cook chilies, garlic and cumin, stirring constantly, 3 minutes. Return beef to Dutch oven. Stir in tomatoes and onion soup mix blended with water. Bring to a boil over high heat. Reduce heat to low and simmer covered, stirring occasionally, 1 hour. Stir in okra, red pepper and corn. Bring to a boil over high heat. Reduce heat to low and simmer covered, stirring occasionally, 30 minutes or until meat is tender. Sprinkle with cilantro.   Makes about 6 servings

Menu Suggestion: Serve with warm crusty bread and sorbet for dessert.

Shrimply Delicious Creole

  2 tablespoons butter or margarine
¾ cup chopped green bell pepper
½ cup chopped celery
  1 can (14½ ounces) whole peeled tomatoes, undrained and chopped
  1 tablespoon finely chopped parsley
  1 envelope Lipton Recipe Secrets Golden Onion Soup Mix
½ cup water
  1 pound uncooked medium shrimp, peeled and deveined

In 12-inch skillet, melt butter over medium heat and cook green pepper with celery until tender. Add tomatoes and parsley, then golden onion soup mix blended with water. Bring to a boil over high heat. Reduce heat to low and simmer covered, stirring occasionally, 20 minutes. Add shrimp and cook 5 minutes or until shrimp turn pink.   Makes about 4 servings

Menu Suggestion: Serve over hot cooked rice with broccoli or asparagus and croissants or hot dinner rolls.

Index